RUMBLE in the JUNGLE

for Oliver

GW00402423

Rumble in the Jungle
Text: Maryam Master
Illustrations and book design: A j Kent
Copyright © Bahá'í Publications Australia – 2007

**Bahá'í
Publications
Australia**

First edition: 2007
All Rights Reserved
ISBN 1 876322 03 9

Distributed by
Bahá'í Distribution Services
P.O. Box 300
Bunddora, Vic 3083 Australia

bds@bahai.org.au
www.bahaibooks.com

Once upon a time, in the heart of the jungle, a little ant called Joseph Henry William Evans the third - or Joe for short - sat down to eat his lunch. But just as he was about to dig into his delicious piece of breadcrumb… Yumola!"

…he heard a thunderous noise.

Thud!

Thud!

Thud!

Was it a storm brewing?

Perhaps an earthquake?

The sound got closer and closer and louder and louder…

THUD!

THUD!

THUD!

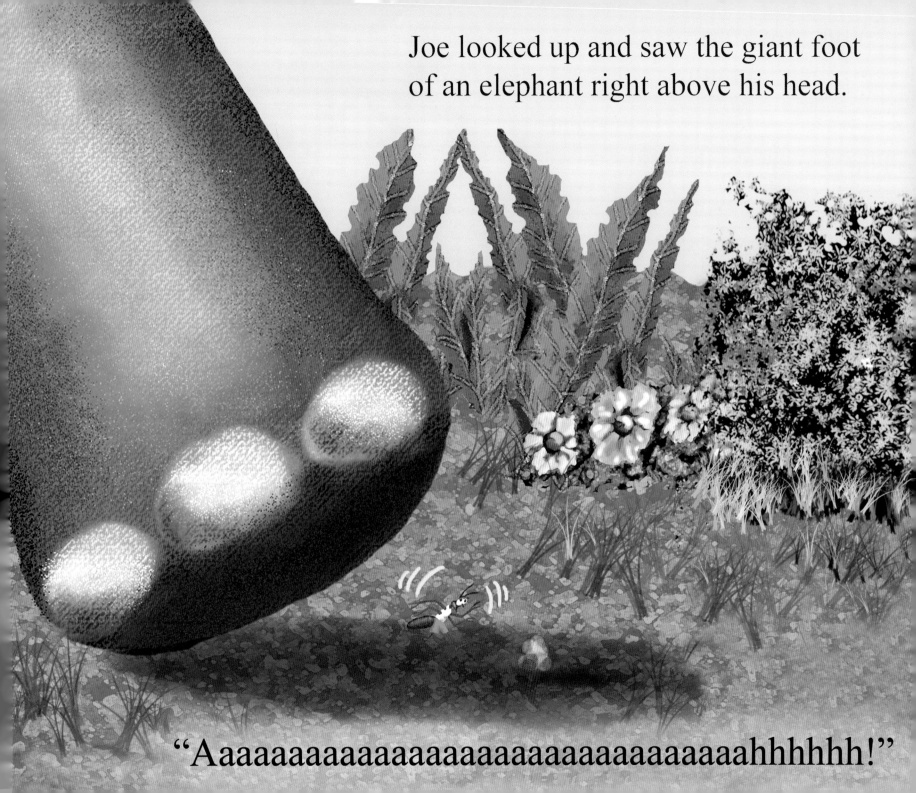

Joe looked up and saw the giant foot
of an elephant right above his head.

"Aaaaaaaaaaaaaaaaaaaaaaaaaaaaaaaaaaaahhhhhh!"

"What was that?!"
said the elephant.

"That was me!"

The gentle elephant,
whose name was Eric,
looked around but
couldn't tell where
this little voice was
coming from.
"Who?"

"Me!! Over here, you great big oaf!"

Eric looked down and finally spotted Joe. "You're tiny!"

"You're HUGE!" replied Joe angrily. "Why don't you watch where you're going! Who said you could stomp around in my jungle anyway?"

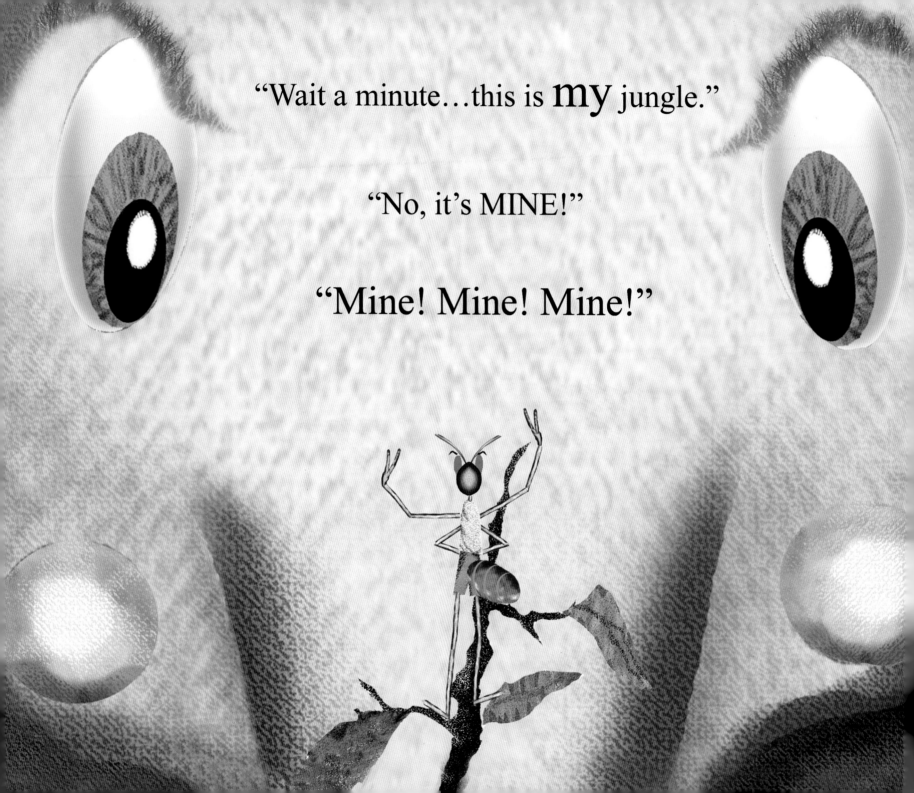

"Now listen," said Joe. "My family's been here for thousands of generations.

We're a big, big, BIG colony.

There's me,
    my 87 sisters, 72 brothers,
       mum, dad, gramps and grandma,
            not to mention millions of
                cousins, aunties and uncles.

This is OUR jungle and OUR home!'

"My family's been here for generations too,"
said Eric.
"My great grandfather built
our home with his very own trunk.

Now, I may not have millions of cousins, but this is still OUR jungle and OUR home!"

"There's only one way to settle this argument." Joe raised his fists and challenged Eric to a fight.

Eric chuckled, "I can't fight you."

"Too chicken, huh? Come on. I may be small, but I'm strong!"

Meanwhile, Grandma Gertrude, the wise old frog from across the river, had overheard them arguing and came to see what the commotion was all about.

"What are you two fighting about?" she said. "God put you in the same universe, the same planet, the same country and the same jungle!

Now it's up to you to live in peace and show friendship to one another."

Joe scoffed. "Ants and elephants can't be friends -
we're sooooo different!" He pointed to Eric's trunk.
"For starters, you have a spectacularly ginormous nose."

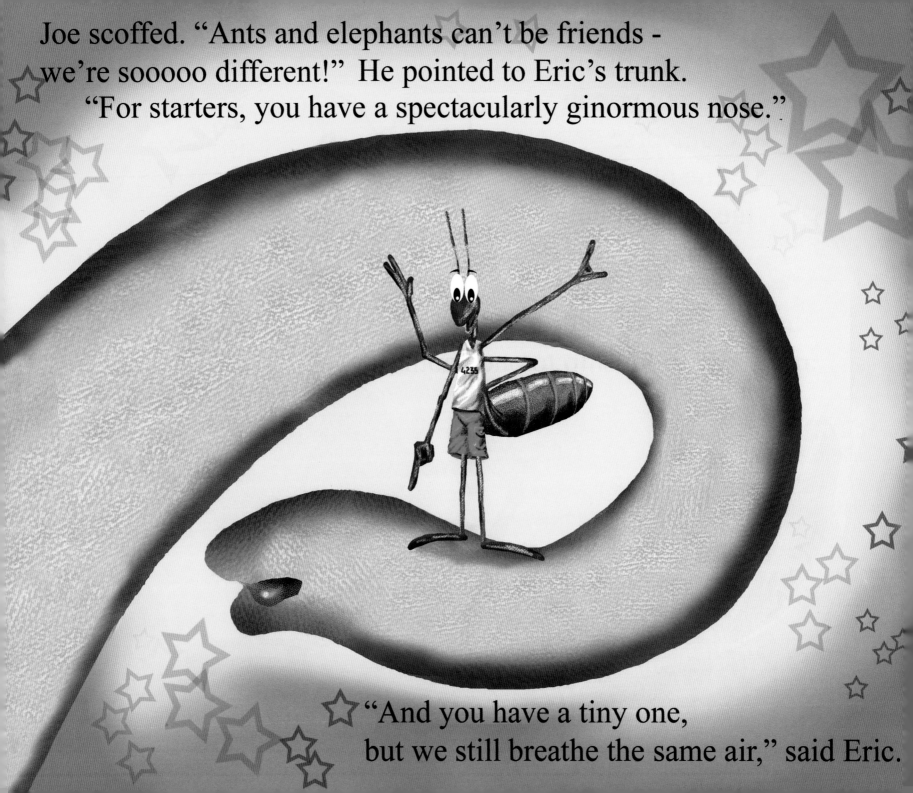

"And you have a tiny one,
but we still breathe the same air," said Eric.

"You have supa dupa floppy ears."
"And you have incy wincy little ones,
but we still hear the same sounds."

"And your eyes…they're simply massive!"
"Yes, but we still see the same things…

...although, I think I've got a better view of the world from up here. You want to take a look?"

Eric lowered his trunk and offered Joe a ride. "Climb aboard."

Joe hopped onto Eric's trunk
and climbed all the way to
the top of his head.

Eric stood up nice and tall
so that Joe could get a full
view of the jungle.

"Wow!" said Joe in amazement. "Look at all the animals!"

He had no idea that the jungle was so vast and the animals so plenty.
There were giraffes, monkeys, tigers, hippos and many, many more.

The jungle looked so beautiful from up above - all those animals living together in peace and harmony.

That's when Joe realised that he was, in fact, part of a much bigger family.

Joe started to think that maybe, just maybe, he and Eric could be friends, despite their great differences.

"If you promise to watch where you're going from now on," Joe said cheekily, "I might consider sharing my lunch with you."

Eric happily accepted Joe's invitation. The two of them sat down to a hearty meal of breadcrumb and chatted for hours and hours and hours.

And that was how the lifelong friendship of Joe the ant and Eric the elephant first began.

Unity

"The earth is but one country and mankind its citizens."
– Bahá'í Faith.

"This is my commandment, that ye love one another,
as I have loved you."
– Christianity.

"And hold you fast to God's bond,
together, and do not scatter."
– Islam.

"Behold how good and how pleasant it is
for brethren to dwell together in unity."
– Jewish Scripture.

"May peace triumph over discord here,
and…reverence over contempt."
– Zoroastrian.